MATRIX

SAINT JULIAN PRESS

POETRY

Praise for MATRIX

Who else but Matt Bialer could make a poem filled with Brontosauruses, New Coke, finding old footage of your girlfriend on YouTube, creamed spinach, and sex ed filmstrips and somehow juggle all of this (and more!) so casually that you don't notice that he's breaking your heart until he has. Bialer is unabashedly direct and clear in the best way; in the minutiae of his life, you will see the reflection of your own life.

—Matthew Rohrer,
The Sky Contains The Plans and *The Others*

Matrix is a deeply moving poem about loss and reconstruction. Matt Bialer is a master of concision and evocation, bringing an incredible palette of nuances to often contradictory feelings. A must-read for all lovers of real-life, raw beautiful poetry.

—Seb Doubinsky
Missing Signal and *The Song Of Synth*

In *Matrix* Bialer's 60th birthday thrusts him into a poetic contemplation on both the striking brevity of life as well as the enduring nature of memory. The readers take a journey moving back and forth through time and the ever-changing landscape of dinosaurs, 35mm film, vinyl records, and other extinct or obsolete objects and beings. Only an 82-million-year-old tooth, set in a matrix of stone, survives like "a footprint across time." The poignancy of grief for his beloved wife's passing and the hopefulness of a new love are vivid reminders that although life is ephemeral, the human capacity to love is undying.

—Loretta Oleck
Paper Chains and *Songs From The Black Hole*

MATRIX

BY

Matt Bialer

SAINT JULIAN PRESS
HOUSTON

Published by
SAINT JULIAN PRESS, Inc.
2053 Cortlandt, Suite 200
Houston, Texas 77008

www.saintjulianpress.com

COPYRIGHT © 2023
TWO THOUSAND AND TWENTY-THREE
©Matt Bialer

ISBN-13: 978-1-955194-19-8
Library of Congress Control Number: 2023940936

Cover Photography: Matt Bialer

MATRIX dedication

For Mary Kathleen Flynn. I met you when I was a widowed 57-year-old just two weeks before Covid lockdown. We were indeed a "wartime romance," as we used to joke. With all the adversity each of us has faced in our lives, it is a miracle that we met. I was not really a believer in fate – until I met you. I don't see living life without you. Thank you for everything.

MATRIX Table of Contents

I.

On the Friday night before my 60th birthday Page 1

It's called Mosasaurus Page 2

The monster of grief Page 18

II.

On Saturday night, I meet Mary Page 21

We are both forward and backward in time Page 25

A footprint across time Page 41

III.

On Sunday morning before my 60th birthday Page 43

I get a call from Mary Page 47

Jiminy Cricket taught me about sex Page 53

IV.

A Carvel ice cream cake is on its way Page 55

Everyone takes a turn Page 57

Hollywood Squares Page 58

"In my beginning is my end. In succession
Houses rise and fall, crumble, are extended,
Are removed, destroyed, restored, or in their place
Is an open field, or a factory, or a by-pass
Old stone to new building, old timber to new fires
Old fire to ashes, and ashes to the earth."

—T.S. Eliot
Four Quartets
"East Coker"
1st Movement

"I'm going to show them a world...without you. A world
without rules and controls, without borders or
boundaries; a world where anything is possible. Where
we go from there is a choice I leave to you."

—Neo in *THE MATRIX*

"Life finds a way."

—Dr. Ian Malcolm
JURASSIC PARK

MATRIX

MATRIX

I.

On the Friday night

Before my 60th birthday

I watch Jurassic World

I've seen the "Park" movies

But not the "World" ones

My girlfriend Mary

And her 20-year-old daughter

Samantha

Suggested that

I should watch Jurassic World

I had replied:

"I don't know

How many variations

Can there be

Of people being

Munched by dinosaurs

And then dumb people

Go back for more?"

Mary replied:

"But they're fun

They're fun"

Okay

I'll give it a whirl

I'm staying home tonight

Because Mary and I

Have a big night out

For my birthday

On Saturday

Even though my birthday

Is actually on Tuesday

But we have other plans

For the night

Of my birthday

Other plans

So I'm resting up

Because turning 60

Makes me feel

Like a dinosaur

A dinosaur

One of the first scenes

Of Jurassic World

Is a big monster water dinosaur

Being fed a Great White Shark

Like it's only

A tasty little snack

I think to myself

That this thing

Must be at least

100 feet long

Bigger than a Blue Whale

Afterwards

I'm curious

I Google

This water dinosaur

I just saw

In the movie

Did it really exist?

The movies have been

Pretty good

About introducing people

To some lesser-known ones

Like Spinosaurus

Or Velociraptor

How many new paleontologists

Have these movies inspired?

The water dinosaur

Did exist

It's called Mosasaurus

And the king of the sea

About 82 to 66 million years ago

In reality it was

About 56 feet long

At its largest

Still much bigger

Than a city bus

And it fed

On prey

Such as sharks

Large fish

Plesiosaurs

And even other Mosasaurs

It was

Not a dinosaur

But a group

Of marine lizards

Like a gigantic Komodo dragon

Or Monitor Lizard

Might have been

Related to snakes

Might have had

A forked tongue

When I was a kid

Dinosaurs were reptiles

The word itself meant

"Terrible Lizard"

I had a favorite

Named Brontosaurus

That doesn't exist anymore

Doesn't exist

It got renamed

Or was actually

Two different dinosaurs

That were no longer lizards

But birds

Discontinued

Like New Coke

I used to play

With toy T-Rexes

And Brontosauruses

And Pluto

Is not a planet anymore

My childhood

Was a lie

Mosasaurus means

"Meuse Lizard"

Referring to the river

Near which

It was first found

One paleontologist

Says though

The movie depiction

Isn't all the way accurate

It's still pretty close

And adds

Like a proud father:

"It's fun

To see Mosasaurus

Finally get

The red-carpet treatment"

The red-carpet treatment

The skull of Mosasaurus

Was equipped

With robust jaws

Capable of swinging

Back and forth

And strong muscles

Capable of powerful bites

Using dozens

Of large teeth

Adopted for cutting prey

Its four limbs

Were shaped

Into mighty paddles

To steer the creature underwater

Its tail was long

And ended

In a downward bend

And a paddle-like fluke

A predator

Possessing excellent vision

To compensate

For its poor sense

Of smell

A high metabolic rate

Suggesting it was endothermic

Or warm-blooded

I ask myself

How do

They know

All of this?

How do

They know?

Had a transatlantic distribution

With its fossils

Found in marine deposits

On both sides

Of the Atlantic Ocean

Including the Midwest

The east coast

Of the United States

Canada

Europe

Turkey

Russia

The Levant

The Africa coastline

From Morocco

To South Africa

Brazil

Argentina

And Antarctica

This guy

Sure got around

When I was a kid

Dinosaurs were reptiles

The word itself meant

"Terrible Lizard"

I had a favorite

Named Brontosaurus

That doesn't exist anymore

Doesn't exist

It got renamed

Or was actually

Two different dinosaurs

That were no longer lizards

But birds

Discontinued

Like New Coke

I used to play

With toy T-Rexes

And Brontosauruses

And Pluto

Is not a planet anymore

I look up

The fossils

Of Mosasaurus

I find a tooth

82 million years old

Set in a matrix

The fine-grained portion

Of a rock

In which

Coarser crystals

Or rock fragments

Are embedded

Or other bone

And teeth fragments

I wonder

How it is possible

For something

To survive

Tens of millions

Of years?

How is it possible?

It's like

A footprint across time

A footprint across time

I remember

How after you died

I felt like

I was now extinct

You certainly were

With friends

And your cousin

We sorted through

Your clothing

And brought 40 large black bags

Of your clothing

To Housing Works

In our neighborhood

In Brooklyn

Black for death

Our now

20-year-old daughter Izzy

Wanted no part

In this operation

No part

She stayed

In her room

So the monster

Of grief

Wouldn't get her

So I was trying

To figure out

What Izzy might want

In the future

She'd want

Something of you

I figured

Something of you

The monster

Of grief

Sometimes

I thought about

Going back

To the store

To see if your clothing

Was still there

On the racks

Excavate you

But I never did

And the store itself

Is now gone

Extinct

I remember

How after

You died

I felt like

I was now extinct

You certainly were

I was struck down

For the first time

In my life

I had no chance

No chance

I once read

That if one is

Confronted by

A Mountain Lion

One's dog

No matter how big

Has no chance

No chance

I had no chance

Against Mosasaurus

The monster

Of grief

Extinct

Not even a tooth

When I was a kid

Dinosaurs were reptiles

The word itself meant

"Terrible Lizard"

I had a favorite

Named Brontosaurus

That doesn't exist anymore

Doesn't exist

It got renamed

Or was actually

Two different dinosaurs

That were no longer lizards

But birds

Discontinued

Like New Coke

I used to play

With toy T-Rexes

And Brontosauruses

And Pluto

Is not a planet anymore

So I'm resting up

Because turning 60

Makes me feel

Like a dinosaur

A dinosaur

A footprint across time

20

II.

On Saturday night

I meet Mary

At Le Gratin

Multi-Michelin star chef

Daniel Boulud's

Brand new restaurant

In the Beekman Hotel

Down in the Financial District

Tiled floors

Crescent leather booths

And banquettes

Vintage mirrors

And art nouveau details

All bathed

In a gentle light

From ceiling-hung globe fixtures

High-set illuminated

Roman numeral clock

That divides the space

Between the front

And the back

With a French menu

Influenced by Lyon

Boulud's hometown

We are both forward

And backward in time

A tooth

82 million years old

Set in a matrix

Situated in

The former site

Of Keith McNally's restaurant

Augustine

Which didn't survive

The Covid pandemic

Didn't survive

No chance

Extinct

Not even a tooth

We order cocktails

And toast

Only the beginning

Of my 60th birthday festivities

Only the beginning

On Tuesday evening

My brother

Sister-in-Law Mary

And nephew Harry

Will come to Brooklyn

All the way from Michigan

And Mary and her daughter

Samantha

And Izzy

And her boyfriend Seamus

Will join

And we'll all have dinner

At a favorite Italian restaurant

In Park Slope

Sotto Voce

And then go to

The Brooklyn Botanic Garden

For a dazzling light show

Called Lightscape

Of course

It's tough

To turn 60

Without you

I could never have imagined

I've reluctantly

Continued my journey

Leaving you behind

Behind

But I am excited

For the future plans

And excited about

The here and now

Of being with Mary

We are both forward

And backward in time

We also toast

The first year

Of Mary's new job

At PEI Group

As Editor-in-Chief

Of PE Hub

She leads the content

And all things

Private equity-related

Especially transactions

Trends

And dealmakers

Mary used to be

Senior Editor/Senior Video Producer

For The Deal

And broadcast Reporter

At CNN and MSNBC

Sometimes

I find old footage

Of Mary on YouTube

And try to imagine

Knowing her

In another time

Another time

The restaurant

Feels like

It is both

In the future

And the past

Some of the décor

Is the same

Some of it

Is different

In the future

And the past

We are both forward

And backward in time

I order

A half dozen oysters

As my appetizer

Mary orders

Oeuf Mimosa

Caviar de Truite

Deviled egg

Trout caviar

Pickled onions

We hold hands

Across the table

Time with Mary

Is precious

Precious

And stands still

Because I lost love

I appreciate it

So much more

Every minute

Every second

I'm proud

That each of us

Is moving forward

And doing it

Together

Together

If somebody

Told me

4 years ago

That I would

Be with someone else

And be so happy

I would have

Never believed them

Never believed them

A footprint across time

As a main course

Mary orders

Loup de Mer Grilles

And Choux de Bruxelles

Sauce Verjus Aux Raisins

Grilled Branzino

Celery root purée

Brussels sprouts

Brown raisin verjus

I order

The roasted duck breast

Which is heavenly

And we share

Épinards a la Crème

Creamed spinach

Which is

Like the best

We've ever tasted

Mary tells them

It's my 60th

So they serve us

A cup of

Delicious chocolate mousse

Afterwards

We explore the hotel

The Beekman

Which has

A great sense of history

The contemporary

And the aura

Of timelessness

Timelessness

Has all three

Rolled into one

The definition

Of a luxury hotel

Transported us

Into another

More glamorous

More beautiful realm

A footprint across time

As architects say

The hotel has great bones

Occupied a landmark

Queen Anne building

From 1881

The height

Of New York's

Early Gilded Age

One of New York's

First skyscrapers

With nine stories

Built in

What is now

The downtown Financial District

Around the same time

As the Brooklyn Bridge

The building

Was then known

As Temple Court

Redbrick

Turreted structure

With a nine-story

Victorian atrium

And pyramidal skylight

The site saw

The debut

Of Shakespeare's Hamlet

In 1871

Was also home

To Clinton Hall

That housed a beautiful library

The interiors

Were recently redesigned

For the hotel

Bookshelves

In the Bar Room

In the atrium

Alongside leather club chairs

Oriental rugs

Portraits of famous authors

Like Edgar Allan Poe

Who used to spend time

In the building

287 high-ceilinged guest rooms

Which ring

The majestic atrium

Original style moldings

Period chandeliers

We're in

Some sort of

Gilded Age/Total Chic Funhouse

We are both forward

And backward in time

A tooth

82 million years old

Set in a matrix

A footprint across time

We look up

At the atrium

Which reminds me

Of a building

I used to live in

In Greenwich Village

When I first met you

Called the Atrium

When I was a kid

Dinosaurs were reptiles

The word itself meant

"Terrible Lizard"

I had a favorite

Named Brontosaurus

That doesn't exist anymore

Doesn't exist

It got renamed

Or was actually

Two different dinosaurs

That were no longer lizards

But birds

Discontinued

Like New Coke

I used to play

With toy T-Rexes

And Brontosauruses

And Pluto

Is not a planet anymore

Extinct

I remember

How after

You died

I felt like

I was now extinct

You certainly were

I was struck down

For the first time

In my life

I had no chance

No chance

I once read
That if one is
Confronted by
A Mountain Lion
One's dog
No matter how big
Has no chance

No chance

I had no chance
Against Mosasaurus

The monster
Of grief

Extinct

Not even a tooth

We watch

All of the people

In the hotel

Sitting in

The Bar Room

Crowded

Because of the holidays

We're in

Some sort of

Gilded Age/Total Chic Funhouse

We are both forward

And backward in time

Like we're

In the 1999

Science fiction movie

The Matrix

A visual effect

Known as Bullet Time

Or Frozen Moment

Dead Time

Flow Motion

Time Slice

In which

The heightened perception

Of certain characters

Is represented

By allowing

The action

Within a shot

To progress

In slow motion

While the camera appears

To move through the scene

At normal speed

Mary and I

Observe the world together

A frozen moment

Bullet Time

Dead Time

Flow motion

A tooth

82 million years old

Set in a matrix

A footprint across time

42

III.

On Sunday morning

Before my 60th birthday

I find a video

Of an interview

With Mary

On YouTube

From July 27, 2008

She has that

Same radiant

And playful smile

Same wisdom

And insight

Beauty inside

And out

Self-confidence

Where was I

On that day?

Where was I?

I sometimes feel
I've always known her
Even though I haven't

Always known her

In the video
She talks about
Creative partnerships
Cropping up
Among online video companies
And traditional video
Meaning television

Talks about
What Dailymotion
Is doing

With user-generated content

People can

Submit their videos

And they might become

A pop-up

"If they see your video

And think

It has pop-up potential

They'll turn it

Into a pop-up video"

Here Mary

Is talking about this

Many years

Before TikTok

Instagram

And Twitter

Where people

Just post their own content

My honey

Is sentient

I see that

Dailymotion

Is still around

But barely

They seem irrelevant

The word itself meant

"Terrible Lizard"

I had a favorite

Named Brontosaurus

That doesn't exist anymore

Doesn't exist

It got renamed

Or was actually

Two different dinosaurs

That were no longer lizards

But birds

Discontinued

Like New Coke

I used to play

With toy T-Rexes

And Brontosauruses

And Pluto

Is not a planet anymore

I get

A call

From Mary

Oh no

She's tested positive

For Covid

She had

Mentioned

A scratchy throat yesterday

I ask her:

"Are you alright?

How do you feel?"

She says

She has a sore throat

And feels tired

But no fever

Symptoms seem mild

At least so far

But this means

She and Samantha

Can't come out

For my birthday

Tuesday night

But I realize

Since I was

Exposed to Mary

Neither can I

Neither can I

My birthday plans

Are out the window

I call my brother

And tell him

Oh well

At home

I wear a mask

Around Izzy

Who's home

From school

Tuesday

My birthday

I don't

Really feel well

But I still test negative

For Covid

If I am going

To get it

I just want

To get it over with

I look at

The birthday cheer

For me on Facebook

I feel loved

My fifth grade

Elementary school teacher writes:

"I can't believe

You're 60"

Ken was young

When he was

My teacher

He's stayed

In touch

With many of his students

I remember

We watched

A filmstrip

About wet dreams

And sex education

The girls were separated

From the boys

"Part 1:

How Life Is Handed On"

A filmstrip

This was

Cutting-edge technology

Nixon was President

A filmstrip

Essentially a series

Of images

On a roll

Of 35-mm film

That was inserted

Into a projector

Allowed teachers

To project one image

At a time

Onto a screen

Accompanied by narration

And music

On a vinyl record

That went "beep"

When it was time

For the next image

A filmstrip

Taught me

About sex

A filmstrip

And I remember

A 16mm Bell & Howell Autoload

Rolled out

Into my classroom

For a film about sex education

Starring Jiminy Cricket

Jiminy Cricket

Taught me

About sex

54

IV.

I get a text

That a Carvel ice cream cake

Is on its way

And I don't need to ask

If it is from Mary

And sure enough

It arrives

I text Mary

And thank her:

"You are so sweet

And thoughtful"

At 6 pm

Mary tells me

To look

For a Zoom link

In my email

She's arranged

A birthday Zoom

With my family

My parents

My brother

And sister-in-law

And nephew

My sister

And her boyfriend

Izzy and her boyfriend

Mary

And Samantha

Zoom

Which has

Pushed out Skype

Everyone

Takes a turn

With a memory

About me

Some of it embarrassing

I would cry

And write miserable letters

From sleepaway camp

I collected Band-Aids and toothpicks

What was my fascination

With Band-Aids?

Mary talks about

My great capacity for love

That it comes from

My parents

And the love

I give to my family

Izzy and to you

And to her

I think of

The old game show

Hollywood Squares

With celebrity contestants

Each in their own squares

Like an onstage Zoom meeting

Paul Lynde

Phyllis Diller

Vincent Price

Joan Rivers

Zsa Zsa Gabor

Charles Nelson Reilly

And Benjamin

The Brontosaurus

All extinct

Discontinued

Like New Coke

I look at

All of us

On Zoom

A different configuration

From when

You were alive

A footprint across time

Most of us

Had never heard

Of Zoom

I look at

All of us

On Zoom

And for

A moment

We all freeze

We're all

In Bullet Time

Or Frozen Moment

Dead Time

Flow Motion

Time Slice

We all freeze

We're all

In Bullet Time

ACKNOWLEDGEMENTS

I would like to thank my daughter Izzy Lapidus for being a great supporter and always making her "Dada" proud. Mary Kathleen Flynn for being my girlfriend and editor, and partner-in-crime. Samantha Quain for telling me to see Jurassic World. Elizabeth Cohen for being a good friend. Seb Doubinsky for being a great friend and reader. Matthew Rohrer for being a guiding light. Loretta Oleck for her support and continuing friendship. And Ron Starbuck, the brilliant publisher and visionary of Saint Julian Press.

ABOUT THE AUTHOR

Matt Bialer is the author of dozens of poetry books, including *VIEW-MASTER LAND* (Finishing Line Press, 2023), *MAZE* (Finishing Line Press, 2021) and *ALWAYS SAY GOODNIGHT* (KYSO Flash, 2020). His poems have also appeared in many print and online journals, including *Retort*, *Le Zaporogue*, *Green Mountains Review*, *Gobbet*, *Forklift Ohio* and *H_NGM_N*. In addition, Matt is an acclaimed black-and-white street photographer who has exhibited his work widely. Some of his images are in the permanent collections of The Brooklyn Museum, The Museum of the City of New York and The New York Public Library. He is also an accomplished watercolor landscape painter with works in many private collections.

Typefaces Used

CALIBRI - Calibri
GARAMOND - Garamond
PERPETUA TILTING MT

Printed in the USA
CPSIA information can be obtained
at www.ICGtesting.com
LVHW022003121023
760666LV00021B/1715